2022 Holidays

JANUARY
1 New Year's Day
6 Epiphany
17 Martin Luther King Jr.'s Birthday, observed

FEBRUARY
1 Lunar New Year (China)
2 Candlemas
2 Groundhog Day
12 Abraham Lincoln's Birthday
14 Valentine's Day
15 National Flag of Canada Day
21 Presidents' Day
22 George Washington's Birthday

MARCH
2 Ash Wednesday
7 Orthodox Lent begins
8 International Women's Day
13 Daylight Saving Time begins at 2:00 A.M.
14 Commonwealth Day (Canada)
17 St. Patrick's Day
20 Vernal Equinox
31 César Chávez Day

APRIL
1 All Fools' Day
2 Ramadan begins at sundown
10 Palm Sunday
15 Good Friday
15 Passover begins at sundown
17 Easter
18 Easter Monday
22 Earth Day
24 Orthodox Easter
29 National Arbor Day

MAY
1 May Day
5 Cinco de Mayo
8 Mother's Day
21 Armed Forces Day
22 National Maritime Day
23 Victoria Day (Canada)
30 Memorial Day

JUNE
5 Whitsunday–Pentecost
5 World Environment Day
12 Orthodox Pentecost
14 Flag Day
19 Father's Day
19 Juneteenth
21 Summer Solstice
21 National Indigenous Peoples Day (Canada)

JULY
1 Canada Day
4 Independence Day
23 National Day of the Cowboy
29 First of Muharram begins at sundown

AUGUST
1 Civic Holiday (Canada)
19 National Aviation Day
26 Women's Equality Day

SEPTEMBER
5 Labor Day
11 Patriot Day
11 Grandparents Day
17 Constitution Day
21 International Day of Peace
22 Autumnal Equinox
25 Rosh Hashanah begins at sundown

OCTOBER
3 Child Health Day
4 Yom Kippur begins at sundown
9 Leif Eriksson Day
10 Columbus Day, observed
10 Indigenous Peoples' Day
10 Thanksgiving Day (Canada)
24 United Nations Day
31 Halloween

NOVEMBER
6 Daylight Saving Time ends at 2:00 A.M.
8 Election Day
10 U.S. Marine Corps Birthday
11 Veterans Day
11 Remembrance Day (Canada)
19 Discovery of Puerto Rico Day
20 National Child Day (Canada)
24 Thanksgiving Day

DECEMBER
7 National Pearl Harbor Remembrance Day
15 Bill of Rights Day
17 Wright Brothers Day
18 Chanukah begins at sundown
21 Winter Solstice
25 Christmas Day
26 First day of Kwanzaa
26 Boxing Day (Canada)
31 New Year's Eve

2022

JANUARY
S	M	T	W	T	F	S
						1
2	3	4	5	6	7	8
9	10	11	12	13	14	15
16	17	18	19	20	21	22
23	24	25	26	27	28	29
30	31					

FEBRUARY
S	M	T	W	T	F	S
		1	2	3	4	5
6	7	8	9	10	11	12
13	14	15	16	17	18	19
20	21	22	23	24	25	26
27	28					

MARCH
S	M	T	W	T	F	S
		1	2	3	4	5
6	7	8	9	10	11	12
13	14	15	16	17	18	19
20	21	22	23	24	25	26
27	28	29	30	31		

APRIL
S	M	T	W	T	F	S
					1	2
3	4	5	6	7	8	9
10	11	12	13	14	15	16
17	18	19	20	21	22	23
24	25	26	27	28	29	30

MAY
S	M	T	W	T	F	S
1	2	3	4	5	6	7
8	9	10	11	12	13	14
15	16	17	18	19	20	21
22	23	24	25	26	27	28
29	30	31				

JUNE
S	M	T	W	T	F	S
			1	2	3	4
5	6	7	8	9	10	11
12	13	14	15	16	17	18
19	20	21	22	23	24	25
26	27	28	29	30		

JULY
S	M	T	W	T	F	S
					1	2
3	4	5	6	7	8	9
10	11	12	13	14	15	16
17	18	19	20	21	22	23
24	25	26	27	28	29	30
31						

AUGUST
S	M	T	W	T	F	S
	1	2	3	4	5	6
7	8	9	10	11	12	13
14	15	16	17	18	19	20
21	22	23	24	25	26	27
28	29	30	31			

SEPTEMBER
S	M	T	W	T	F	S
				1	2	3
4	5	6	7	8	9	10
11	12	13	14	15	16	17
18	19	20	21	22	23	24
25	26	27	28	29	30	

OCTOBER
S	M	T	W	T	F	S
						1
2	3	4	5	6	7	8
9	10	11	12	13	14	15
16	17	18	19	20	21	22
23	24	25	26	27	28	29
30	31					

NOVEMBER
S	M	T	W	T	F	S
		1	2	3	4	5
6	7	8	9	10	11	12
13	14	15	16	17	18	19
20	21	22	23	24	25	26
27	28	29	30			

DECEMBER
S	M	T	W	T	F	S
				1	2	3
4	5	6	7	8	9	10
11	12	13	14	15	16	17
18	19	20	21	22	23	24
25	26	27	28	29	30	31

Flip to the back for a look ahead with the 2023 Advance Planner.

January

**JANUARY 17:
FULL WOLF MOON**

GOALS AND DREAMS:

_____
_____
_____
_____
_____
_____
_____
_____
_____
_____
_____
_____
_____
_____
_____
_____
_____

*And now let us
believe in a long year
that is given to us,
new, untouched, full
of things that have
never been.*

–Rainer Maria Rilke,
Bohemian-Austrian poet
(1875–1926)

SUNDAY	MONDAY	TUESDAY
2	3	4
9	10	11
16	17 *Martin Luther King Jr.'s Birthday, observed*	18
23	24	25
30	31	

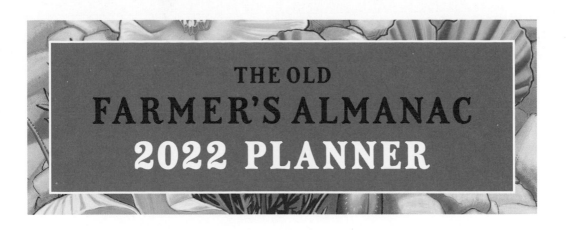

THE OLD
FARMER'S ALMANAC
2022 PLANNER

Begin the new year square with every man.

–Robert B. Thomas, founder of
The Old Farmer's Almanac (1766–1846)

A PLANNER FILLED WITH FUN FACTS, LORE, AND MORE!

PUBLISHER: Sherin Pierce

EDITORIAL: Benjamin Kilbride, *writer;* Heidi Stonehill, *editor;* Catherine Boeckmann,
Christopher Burnett, Jack Burnett, Sarah Perreault, Janice Stillman

ART DIRECTOR: Colleen Quinnell

PRODUCTION: David Ziarnowski, *director;* Brian Johnson, *manager;*
Jennifer Freeman, Rachel Kipka, Janet Selle

Astronomical events are given in Eastern Time.

ILLUSTRATIONS: Kristin Kest

If you find this calendar, please return it to:

Name

Address

Phone (Home)   (Work)   (Cell)

Printed in China by R. R. Donnelley

ISBN: 978-1-57198-902-4

ASK A FRIEND FOR SUPPORT AND ENCOURAGEMENT TO MEET YOUR GOALS.

WEDNESDAY	THURSDAY	FRIDAY	SATURDAY
			1 *New Year's Day*
5	6 *Epiphany*	7	8
12	13	14	15
19	20	21	22
26	27	28	29

For more holidays and Moon phases, see the weekly pages that follow.

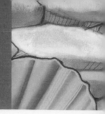

27 MONDAY

The 134-mile-wide
Galle Crater on Mars
has ridges that appear
to form a smiling face.

28 TUESDAY

Who doffs his coat
on a winter's day,
Will gladly put it on
in May.

29 WEDNESDAY

*You can't be brave
if you've only
had wonderful things
happen to you.*
–Mary Tyler Moore,
American actress
(1936–2017)

30 THURSDAY

The northern
cardinal is the state
bird of Illinois,
Indiana, Kentucky,
North Carolina, Ohio,
Virginia, and
West Virginia.

On New Year's Eve
in Romania, people
dress up as bears
and visit other
people's homes to
scare away evil spirits.

FRIDAY 31

New Year's Day

*To welcome in the
newborn year,
A thousand
happy voices
Are heard in tones of
mirthful cheer,
And every heart rejoices.*
–The Country Gentleman,
1854

SATURDAY 1

SUNDAY 2

NEW MOON

REMINDERS

January

3 MONDAY

New Year's resolution chuckle: Plan to be more spontaneous.

4 TUESDAY

Time to get out the seed catalogs.

5 WEDNESDAY

Keep to moderation, keep the end in view, follow nature.
–Marcus Annaeus Lucanus, Roman poet (A.D. 39–65)

6 THURSDAY

Epiphany
At twelfth day, the days are lengthened a cock's stride.

The potato was
the first food to
be successfully grown
in space.

FRIDAY 7

Elvis Presley's Birthday

*Truth is like the sun.
You can shut it out
for a time, but it ain't
goin' away.*

–Elvis Presley, American
entertainer (1935–77)

SATURDAY 8

FIRST QUARTER

SUNDAY 9

REMINDERS

10 MONDAY

A daymark is the unique markings of a lighthouse tower that identify it during daylight hours.

11 TUESDAY

If you wear a hairpin in your shoe, you will meet a good friend.

12 WEDNESDAY

A pony is a full-grown horse that is no taller than 14.2 hands.

13 THURSDAY

On this day in 1886, a sudden blizzard hit Kansas, taking the lives of 80 percent of the cattle in the state.

FRIDAY **14**

The ostrich has the largest eye of any land animal, measuring 2 inches in diameter.

SATURDAY **15**

Shake and shake the catsup bottle. None will come, and then a lot'll.
–Richard Armour, American poet (1906–89)

SUNDAY **16**

A clean conscience makes a soft pillow.

REMINDERS

January

17 MONDAY

FULL WOLF MOON

**Martin Luther King
Jr.'s Birthday, observed**

**Benjamin Franklin's
Birthday**

18 TUESDAY

*We may have all
come on different ships,
but we're in the same
boat now.*
–Martin Luther King Jr.,
American civil rights leader
(1929–68)

19 WEDNESDAY

Clear Moon,
Frost soon.

20 THURSDAY

*If you do not tell the
truth about yourself,
you can not tell it about
other people.*
–Virginia Woolf, English
writer (1882–1941)

Start planning your
garden now so that
you are ready when it
is time to plant.

FRIDAY 21

About 4 percent of
all cheese is stolen,
making it the most
pilfered food on Earth.

SATURDAY 22

Even the ant has its bite.
–Turkish proverb

SUNDAY 23

REMINDERS

January

24 MONDAY

If herbs are about to go bad, freeze them whole to save them for later.

25 TUESDAY

LAST QUARTER

26 WEDNESDAY

Colors seen by candlelight will not seem the same by day.
–Elizabeth Barrett Browning, English poet (1806–61)

27 THURSDAY

On this day in 2019, International Falls, Minnesota, experienced record cold when temperatures plummeted to –47°F.

Better to ask twice than to
   lose your way once.

FRIDAY 28

The Great Frigatebird
   can fly for months
   without landing,
sleeping for only 7 to
12 seconds at a time.

SATURDAY 29

   In Scotland, there
   are 421 words
   and expressions
   about snow.

SUNDAY 30

REMINDERS

February

**FEBRUARY 16:
FULL SNOW MOON**

GOALS AND DREAMS:

_____
_____
_____
_____
_____
_____
_____
_____
_____
_____
_____
_____
_____
_____
_____
_____

*The way to be
truly happy is to
fill up every
passing hour with
something useful.*
–The Old Farmer's
Almanac, 1873

SUNDAY	MONDAY	TUESDAY
		1 *Lunar New Year (China)*
6	7	8
13	14 *Valentine's Day*	15 *National Flag of Canada Day*
20	21 *Presidents' Day*	22 *George Washington's Birthday*
27	28	

KEEP A JOURNAL OF YOUR THOUGHTS; INSIGHTS MAY FOLLOW.

WEDNESDAY	THURSDAY	FRIDAY	SATURDAY
2 *Candlemas* *Groundhog Day*	3	4	5
9	10	11	12 *Abraham Lincoln's* *Birthday*
16	17	18	19
23	24	25	26

For more holidays and Moon phases, see the weekly pages that follow.

31 MONDAY

According to one study, cows that have names produce more milk than unnamed cows.

1 TUESDAY

NEW MOON

Lunar New Year (China)

2 WEDNESDAY

Candlemas
Groundhog Day

Tact is, after all, a kind of mind reading.
–Sarah Orne Jewett, American writer (1849–1909)

3 THURSDAY

Wolves can go for over a week without eating.

FRIDAY 4

You might know what a spork is (spoon and fork combined), but you might not be familiar with these other hybrids: knork (knife and fork), spife (knife and spoon), and sporf (knife, fork, and spoon).

SATURDAY 5

A little kindness from person to person is better than a vast love for all humankind.
–Richard Dehmel, German writer (1863–1920)

SUNDAY 6

To avoid teary eyes, cut onions under cold running water.

REMINDERS

February

7 MONDAY

A poor excuse is better
than none at all.

8 TUESDAY

FIRST QUARTER

9 WEDNESDAY

According to his
granddaughter,
American mobster
Ralph "Bottles"
Capone (brother of
Al Capone) lobbied to
have milk bottles state
when they had been
bottled so that buyers
could judge freshness.

10 THURSDAY

If snails come out in
February, they will stay
home in March.

Between the optimist and the pessimist, the difference is droll: The optimist sees the doughnut; the pessimist, the hole!
–Oscar Wilde, Irish writer (1854–1900)

FRIDAY 11

Abraham Lincoln's Birthday

On this day in 1914, construction began on the Lincoln Memorial in Washington, D.C.

SATURDAY 12

The sharper the blast,
The sooner it's past.

SUNDAY 13

REMINDERS

February

14 MONDAY

Valentine's Day

The phrase "wear your heart on your sleeve" may have started in the Middle Ages, when jousting knights wore scarves or ribbons from their ladies.

15 TUESDAY

National Flag of Canada Day

Susan B. Anthony's Birthday (Fla.)

Everyone has a gift for something, even if it is the gift of being a good friend.
–Marian Anderson, American singer (1897–1993)

16 WEDNESDAY

FULL SNOW MOON

17 THURSDAY

While the Moon appears round to viewers on Earth, it is in fact slightly egg-shape.

Sinuses congested?
Add a good
dose of horseradish
to your sandwich.

FRIDAY 18

Content makes poor men
rich; discontent makes
rich men poor.

SATURDAY 19

On average, a person
will shed about
105 pounds of skin by
the time they are 70.

SUNDAY 20

REMINDERS

Complement this planner with daily weather and Almanac wit and wisdom at Almanac.com.

February

21 MONDAY

Presidents' Day
Family Day (Alta., B.C., N.B., Ont., Sask.)

In 1943, Dwight D. Eisenhower (a WWII general at the time) became the only future U.S. president to be knighted by England.

22 TUESDAY

George Washington's Birthday

Labor to keep alive in your breast that little spark of celestial fire—conscience.

–George Washington, 1st U.S. president (1732–99)

23 WEDNESDAY

LAST QUARTER

24 THURSDAY

"Snow creep" is the continuous, extremely slow, downhill movement of a layer of snow.

Heritage Day (Y.T.)

The "gold" in 'Yukon
Gold' potatoes,
developed in Canada,
comes not only from
the Yukon River
and gold rush country
but also their
yellow flesh.

FRIDAY **25**

---

*The critical period
in matrimony
is breakfast-time.*
–Sir Alan Patrick Herbert,
English writer (1890–1971)

SATURDAY **26**

The more rain, the
more rest;
Fair weather's not
always best.

SUNDAY **27**

REMINDERS

March

**MARCH 18:
FULL WORM MOON**

GOALS AND DREAMS:

_____
_____
_____
_____
_____
_____
_____
_____
_____
_____
_____
_____
_____
_____
_____
_____

*When you have
confidence, you can
have a lot of fun;
and when you have
fun, you can do
amazing things.*
–Joe Namath, American
football player (b. 1943)

SUNDAY	MONDAY	TUESDAY
		1
6	7 *Orthodox Lent begins*	8 *International Women's Day*
13 *Daylight Saving Time begins at 2:00 A.M.*	14 *Commonwealth Day (Canada)*	15
20 *Vernal Equinox*	21	22
27	28	29

CHALLENGE YOUR MIND WITH PUZZLES OR CARD GAMES.

WEDNESDAY	THURSDAY	FRIDAY	SATURDAY
2 *Ash Wednesday*	3	4	5
9	10	11	12
16	17 *St. Patrick's Day*	18	19
23	24	25	26
30	31 *César Chávez Day*		

For more holidays and Moon phases, see the weekly pages that follow.

28 MONDAY

In ancient times, butter-filled containers were commonly buried in Irish peat bogs, possibly as a way to preserve the food, enhance its flavor, or deter theft. "Bog butter" can still be found to this day.

1 TUESDAY

Mardi Gras (Ala., La.)
Town Meeting Day (Vt.)

Find a plastic baby inside your king cake? According to one Mardi Gras tradition, you must bake this frosted treat for friends the following year.

2 WEDNESDAY

NEW MOON

Ash Wednesday
Texas Independence Day

3 THURSDAY

To remove rusty screws or bolts, presoak them in lemon juice or cola.

If we could sell our experiences for what they cost us, we'd all be millionaires.

–Abigail Van Buren, American advice columnist (1918–2013)

FRIDAY 4

Sea otters sleep on their backs in the water, wrapping themselves in seaweed to avoid floating away.

SATURDAY 5

Fire whirls, aka fire devils or firenadoes, are tornado-like whirlwinds of fire and ash caused by wildfires.

SUNDAY 6

REMINDERS

March

7 MONDAY

Orthodox Lent begins

Cold rice and cold tea are
bearable, but cold looks
and cold words are not.
–Japanese proverb

8 TUESDAY

**International
Women's Day**

Sure [Fred Astaire] *was
great, but … Ginger
Rogers did everything
he did backwards—
and in high heels.*
–attributed to Bob Thaves,
American cartoonist
(1924–2006)

9 WEDNESDAY

When eating soup,
hold your spoon
like a pencil and dip it
away from you.

10 THURSDAY

FIRST QUARTER

---

*Is yon strange creature
a common chickadee,
Or a migrant alouette
from Picardy* [France]?
–Ogden Nash, American
writer (1902–71)

FRIDAY 11

Freeze leftover wine
or broth in ice cube
trays to use later
in sauces and soups.

SATURDAY 12

**Daylight Saving Time
begins at 2:00 A.M.**

*Even if a farmer intends
to loaf, he gets up
in time to get an
early start.*
–Edgar Watson Howe,
American writer
(1853–1937)

SUNDAY 13

REMINDERS

Complement this planner with daily weather and Almanac wit and wisdom at Almanac.com.

March

14 MONDAY

Commonwealth Day (Canada)

The Commonwealth of Nations has 54 member countries from Africa, the Americas, Asia, Europe, and the Pacific.

15 TUESDAY

The oldest fabric, thought to be linen, originated around 7000 B.C.

16 WEDNESDAY

The Hoatzin (aka stinkbird), a native of South America, gets its name from the smell of the bacterial fermentation that occurs in its stomach.

17 THURSDAY

St. Patrick's Day

Evacuation Day (Suffolk Co., Mass.)

A house can't be kept without talk.

–Irish proverb

FULL WORM MOON

SATURDAY 19

Q: What's the
definition of
"vitamin"?
A: It's what you do
when a friend comes
to the door.

SUNDAY 20

Vernal Equinox

*Though the groundhog
and crocus creep
into their holes,
It's Spring, and the
almanac shows it!*

–Robert Jones Burdette,
American clergyman and
humorist (1844–1914)

REMINDERS

March

21 MONDAY

In the 1890s, the U.S. Supreme Court named the tomato a vegetable for tax purposes, despite its being a fruit.

22 TUESDAY

On this day in 1920, the northern lights were visible as far south as Bradenton, Florida.

23 WEDNESDAY

Today is a good time to repot houseplants.

24 THURSDAY

The term "pound cake" came from the original recipes calling for a pound each of butter, eggs, and sugar.

LAST QUARTER

FRIDAY 25

SATURDAY 26

Seeing a redbird
on Saturday means that
your sweetheart will
arrive soon.

SUNDAY 27

*Spring in the world!
And all things are
made new!*
–Richard Hovey, American
poet (1864–1900)

REMINDERS

28 MONDAY

Seward's Day (Alaska)
Alaska hosts more than 40 active volcanoes.

29 TUESDAY

To prevent brown sugar from becoming hard, place a marshmallow in its container.

30 WEDNESDAY

Expect rain if hens spread and ruffle their tail feathers.

31 THURSDAY

César Chávez Day
Stay on top of weeds: A few times per week, spend 10 to 15 minutes pulling them out.

FRIDAY 1

NEW MOON

All Fools' Day

SATURDAY 2

Ramadan begins at sundown

Pascua Florida Day

In the tropics, the skins of ripe oranges are green because the chlorophyll in them is not killed by cooling temperatures to reveal orange pigment.

SUNDAY 3

Sometimes a fool makes a good suggestion.
–Nicolas Boileau-Despréaux, French poet (1636–1711)

REMINDERS

April

**APRIL 16:
FULL PINK MOON**

GOALS AND DREAMS:

_____
_____
_____
_____
_____
_____
_____
_____
_____
_____
_____
_____
_____
_____
_____
_____
_____
_____

*Love the world as
your own self;
then you can truly
care for all things.*
–Lao-tzu, Chinese
philosopher
(6th century)

SUNDAY	MONDAY	TUESDAY
3	4	5
10	11	12
Palm Sunday		
17	18	19
Easter	*Easter Monday*	
24	25	26
Orthodox Easter		

BE MINDFUL OF CONSEQUENCES.

WEDNESDAY	THURSDAY	FRIDAY	SATURDAY
		1 *All Fools' Day*	2 *Ramadan begins at sundown*
6	7	8	9
13	14	15 *Good Friday* *Passover begins at sundown*	16
20	21	22 *Earth Day*	23
27	28	29 *National Arbor Day*	30

For more holidays and Moon phases, see the weekly pages that follow.

April

4 MONDAY

A raindrop can
fall at speeds up to
18 miles per hour.

5 TUESDAY

Yellow streaks in
sunset sky,
Wind and daylong
rain are nigh.

6 WEDNESDAY

The human brain
can remember
about 50,000
individual scents.

7 THURSDAY

In the 1630s, some
Dutch investors
valued tulips more
than gold.

FRIDAY 8

Long Acre Square was renamed Times Square in April 1904, during construction of a new building that would serve as headquarters for *The New York Times.* The company moved there in January 1905.

SATURDAY 9

FIRST QUARTER

SUNDAY 10

𝔓alm 𝔖unday

Palm leaves blessed during Christian services today may be burned later, the ashes to be used during Ash Wednesday services in the following year.

REMINDERS

April

11 MONDAY

Lightning nearby? Drop anything metal (golf club, bike, or fishing pole) and seek shelter inside an enclosed building or car. Avoid bodies of water, open fields, hilltops, and tall, isolated objects (such as trees).

12 TUESDAY

There can not be a crisis next week. My schedule is already full.
–Henry Alfred Kissinger, American diplomat (b. 1923)

13 WEDNESDAY

Thomas Jefferson's Birthday

Thomas Jefferson invented a wheel cipher for encoding messages.

14 THURSDAY

Use beets or cranberries to make your own pink Easter egg dye.

FRIDAY 15

Good Friday
**Passover begins
at sundown**

Freedom is above
silver and gold.

SATURDAY 16

FULL PINK MOON

SUNDAY 17

Easter
*Joy and peace we
have in Thee,
Now and through
eternity.*
–Horatius Bonar, Scottish
clergyman (1808–89)

REMINDERS

April

18 MONDAY

Easter Monday
Patriots Day
(Maine, Mass.)

A merry companion is
music on a journey.

19 TUESDAY

Dolphins sleep
with half their brain
shut down and one eye
open in a state called
"unihemispheric
sleep."

20 WEDNESDAY

Research shows that
writing a thank-you
letter both improves
the recipient's
happiness and puts
the writer in more
positive spirits.

21 THURSDAY

San Jacinto Day (Tex.)

Houston, Texas,
is named for Sam
Houston, who led
Texan forces against
the Mexican army
in the pivotal Battle
of San Jacinto (1836)
during the Texas
Revolution.

Earth Day

In 1935, venomous
cane toads were
released into
Australia to control
a beetle infestation.
Now these invasive
toads are wreaking
havoc on fragile
ecosystems there.

LAST QUARTER

Orthodox Easter

**Birthday of Robert B.
Thomas, founder of *The
Old Farmer's Almanac***

Orthodox Easter
can be as late as
May 8 in the
Gregorian calendar
(April 25, Julian).

REMINDERS

_____

_____

_____

_____

_____

_____

25 MONDAY

St. George's Day, observed (N.L.)

When New York was a swamp, we were growing daisies in Newfoundland.
–Joseph R. Smallwood, 1st premier of Newfoundland (1900–91)

26 TUESDAY

The ancient Romans built the first-known greenhouses.

27 WEDNESDAY

I've been on a diet for 2 weeks, and all I've lost is 2 weeks.
–Totie Fields, American comedienne (1930–78)

28 THURSDAY

On this day in 2020, baseball-size hail fell on Marlow, Oklahoma.

National Arbor Day

FRIDAY 29

According to Jewish tradition, tree planting takes place on Tu B'Shevat, called the "New Year of the Trees" or "Jewish Arbor Day," which occurs in January or February (15th day of Shevat).

SATURDAY 30

NEW MOON

Partial Solar Eclipse (not visible in N.Am.)

May Day

SUNDAY 1

It is bad luck to sew or darn on a Sunday.

REMINDERS

Complement this planner with daily weather and Almanac wit and wisdom at Almanac.com.

May

MAY 16:
FULL FLOWER MOON

GOALS AND DREAMS:

_____
_____
_____
_____
_____
_____
_____
_____
_____
_____
_____
_____
_____
_____
_____
_____
_____
_____
_____

Nothing is worth more than this day.
–Johann Wolfgang von Goethe, German poet (1749–1832)

SUNDAY	MONDAY	TUESDAY
1 *May Day*	2	3
8 *Mother's Day*	9	10
15	16	17
22 *National Maritime Day*	23 *Victoria Day (Canada)*	24
29	30 *Memorial Day*	31

DON'T GET DISCOURAGED: USE SLIPUPS AS MOTIVATION TO GET BACK ON TRACK.

WEDNESDAY	THURSDAY	FRIDAY	SATURDAY
4	5	6	7
	Cinco de Mayo		
11	12	13	14
18	19	20	21
			Armed Forces Day
25	26	27	28

For more holidays and Moon phases, see the weekly pages that follow.

May

2 MONDAY

The flowers on fig trees are carnivorous, trapping insects that pollinate them.

3 TUESDAY

Happiness is good health and a bad memory.
–Ingrid Bergman, Swedish actress (1915–82)

4 WEDNESDAY

Expect good luck if a fly falls into your drinking glass.

5 THURSDAY

Cinco de Mayo

The ancient Mayans honored wild turkeys as vessels of the gods.

A false friend and a
shadow stay only while
the Sun shines.

FRIDAY 6

---

*Sometimes the
strength of motherhood
is greater than
natural laws.*
–Barbara Kingsolver,
American writer (b. 1955)

SATURDAY 7

FIRST QUARTER

**Mother's Day
Truman Day (Mo.)**

SUNDAY 8

REMINDERS

Complement this planner with daily weather and Almanac wit and wisdom at Almanac.com.

May

9 MONDAY

Plant lovage throughout your garden to improve the health and flavor of other plants.

10 TUESDAY

A dream of daisies in spring means good luck.

11 WEDNESDAY

Mountains are Earth's undecaying monuments.
–Nathaniel Hawthorne, American writer (1804–64)

12 THURSDAY

The fear of peanut butter becoming stuck to the roof of your mouth is called arachibutyrophobia.

It is not who is right, but what is right, that is of importance.
–Thomas H. Huxley, English biologist (1825–95)

FRIDAY 13

Bamboo can grow up to 35 inches in one day, making it the fastest-growing woody plant in the world.

SATURDAY 14

Total Lunar Eclipse begins (visible in parts of N.Am.)

The ancient Incas believed that a lunar eclipse was caused by a jaguar attacking the Moon.

SUNDAY 15

REMINDERS

Complement this planner with daily weather and Almanac wit and wisdom at Almanac.com.

May

16 MONDAY

FULL FLOWER MOON

17 TUESDAY

*There is a sight all
hearts beguiling—
A youthful mother to
her infant smiling.*

–Joanna Baillie, Scottish
dramatist (1762–1851)

18 WEDNESDAY

Ancient Egyptian
laborers were
paid in radishes.

19 THURSDAY

Stained teeth?
Brush them with
mashed strawberries
and baking soda.

FRIDAY 20

It is one of my sources of happiness never to desire a knowledge of other people's business.
–Dolley Madison, U.S. First Lady (1768–1849)

SATURDAY 21

Armed Forces Day

Take calculated risks. That is quite different from being rash.
–George S. Patton Jr., American army general (1885–1945)

SUNDAY 22

☆ ☆
LAST QUARTER

National Maritime Day

REMINDERS

May

23 MONDAY

Victoria Day (Canada)

*When life seems hard,
the courageous do
not lie down and accept
defeat. Instead, they
are all the more
determined to struggle
for a better future.*
–Queen Elizabeth II, British
monarch (b. 1926)

24 TUESDAY

When saturated
colors of orange and
blue are placed next
to each other, they
appear to vibrate.

25 WEDNESDAY

*My schoolroom lies on
the meadow wide,
Where under the clover
the sunbeams hide.*
–Katharine Lee Bates,
American writer
(1859–1929)

26 THURSDAY

Every slip is not a fall.

Ducks sleep together side by side, with those at the end keeping one eye open to look out for danger.

A 30-milliliter bottle of Chanel No. 5 perfume requires 1,000 jasmine flowers and a dozen roses to make.

Evening red and morning gray speed the traveler on his way. Evening gray and morning red bring down the rain upon his head.

REMINDERS

Complement this planner with daily weather and Almanac wit and wisdom at Almanac.com.

June

JUNE 14:
FULL STRAWBERRY
MOON

GOALS AND DREAMS:

_____
_____
_____
_____
_____
_____
_____
_____
_____
_____
_____
_____
_____
_____
_____
_____
_____
_____
_____

*Cherish your human
connections: your
relationships with
friends and family.*
–Barbara Bush, U.S.
First Lady (1925–2018)

SUNDAY	MONDAY	TUESDAY
5 *Whitsunday–Pentecost* *World Environment Day*	6	7
12 *Orthodox Pentecost*	13	14 *Flag Day*
19 *Father's Day* *Juneteenth*	20	21 *Summer Solstice* *National Indigenous* *Peoples Day (Canada)*
26	27	28

SPEND TIME TOGETHER WITH FAMILY: LISTEN, COMMUNICATE, AND PARTICIPATE.

WEDNESDAY	THURSDAY	FRIDAY	SATURDAY
1	2	3	4
8	9	10	11
15	16	17	18
22	23	24	25
29	30		

JUNE

For more holidays and Moon phases, see the weekly pages that follow.

May–June

30 MONDAY

NEW MOON

Memorial Day

31 TUESDAY

The original name of Memorial Day—Decoration Day—marked a time when people honored fallen soldiers by decorating their graves with flags and flowers.

1 WEDNESDAY

Native to the Indo-Pacific, the regal blue tang *(Paracanthurus hepatus)* is a type of surgeonfish named for the sharp, scalpel-like spine on both sides of its tail.

2 THURSDAY

A copper penny taped to your navel is said to cure seasickness.

Every path hath a puddle.

In 2017, Ed Currie's Smokin' Ed's 'Carolina Reaper' set a world record for being the hottest chile pepper, testing at an average of 1,641,183 Scoville Heat Units. (A jalapeño measures about 2,500 to 8,000 SHU.)

Whitsunday—Pentecost

World Environment Day

Save paper:
Sign up for e-billing.

REMINDERS

June

6 MONDAY

Follow the first law of holes: If you are in one, stop digging.
–Denis Healey, English statesman (1917–2015)

7 TUESDAY

FIRST QUARTER

8 WEDNESDAY

On this day in 1966, a tornado in Topeka, Kansas, tore a 22-mile path while causing $200 million in damage.

9 THURSDAY

Corn belongs to the grass family.

FRIDAY 10

Reuse pickle brine to make refrigerator pickles: Boil brine and then pour over carrots, cucumbers, onions, or radishes in a jar. Seal and let sit in the fridge for at least a day (toss out if brine is murky). Do not reuse brine.

SATURDAY 11

King Kamehameha I Day (Hawaii)

The largest unbranched flower in the world is the titan arum *(Amorphophallus titanium),* which can reach up to 15 feet tall.

SUNDAY 12

Orthodox Pentecost

A good neighbor, a found treasure.

REMINDERS

June

13 MONDAY

For a flag to be flown at half-mast, it should first be raised completely and then lowered to halfway.

14 TUESDAY

FULL STRAWBERRY MOON

Flag Day

15 WEDNESDAY

The "seeds" on the exterior of a strawberry are actually the true fruit, called "achenes." Each of the approximately 200 achenes contains one seed.

16 THURSDAY

There isn't much that tastes better than praise from those who are wise and capable.
–Selma Lagerlof, Swedish writer (1858–1940)

**Bunker Hill Day
(Suffolk Co., Mass.)**

If a ladybug lands on you,
    you'll have good luck.

FRIDAY 17

Some snails can sleep
    for up to 3 years.

SATURDAY 18

**Father's Day
Juneteenth**

*I have found much
happiness in life,
because* [my father]
*taught me where
happiness could be
found.*

–Edgar Guest, English-born
American poet (1881–1959)

SUNDAY 19

REMINDERS

June

20 MONDAY

LAST QUARTER

West Virginia Day

21 TUESDAY

Summer Solstice

National Indigenous Peoples Day (Canada)

The summer night is like a perfection of thought.

–Wallace Stevens, American poet (1879–1955)

22 WEDNESDAY

To prevent your steaks from curling on the grill, score the outer layer of fat at 1-inch intervals.

23 THURSDAY

Do not speak of secrets in a field that is full of little hills.

–Hebrew proverb

Get a Free Bonus Gift!

How would you like to receive next year's elegant Planner (formerly titled Engagement Calendar) PLUS a FREE BONUS GIFT?!

Plus, receive a
FREE BONUS GIFT
with your order!

The Old Farmer's Almanac Planner is a stylish and handy companion that you can count on to manage your daily appointments and activities. It is also an ideal place to record your daily observations and inspirations. Each day offers a little bit of wit or wisdom to enjoy.

Order now to ensure that you have your 2023 planner when you need it! PLUS, you get a Free Bonus Gift with your order.

Due to mailing requirements, this offer is only available in the United States.

PLANNER REORDER FORM

☐ **Send me the 2023 Planner, plus my FREE gift!** (Includes renewal plan)*

Please print:

Name_____

Street_____

City/State/Zip_____

☐ Check enclosed   Charge my: ☐ Visa ☐ MasterCard ☐ AmEx ☐ Discover

Acct. #_____ Exp. date_____ Sec. code #_____

Signature _____
            (Required for credit card orders)
Email_____

The Old Farmer's Almanac 2023 Planner	
Qty. planners ordered	_____
x $14.99	$_____
Add state sales tax**	$_____
U.S. s & h add	$ 6.95
Total enclosed	$_____
Key code: A2PLN03	

THREE EASY WAYS TO ORDER! (U.S. customers only)

✉ **MAIL form with payment to:** The Old Farmer's Almanac/Planner, P.O. Box 520, Dublin, NH 03444-0520

☎ **PHONE:** Call toll-free 1-800-ALMANAC (1-800-256-2622)

🖱 **ONLINE:** Visit Almanac.com/Shop

*Enter my guaranteed reservation for all future editions of The Old Farmer's Almanac Planner at the lowest price available. I will get a BONUS gift every time, just for looking. Next July, I will receive an advance notice of shipment of the 2024 planner and my BONUS gift. NO OBLIGATION! I may use that card to change my address, change my order, or cancel next year's shipment. I am under no obligation to purchase future planners and may cancel at any time.

**Residents of MA, IL, and IN: Please add applicable sales tax (current rate or 6.25% will be accepted).

Planner will ship in August.   A2PLN03

Name: _____

Address: _____

_____

City/Town: _____ State: _____ Zip: _____

The Old Farmer's Almanac/Planner
PO Box 520
Dublin, NH 03444-0520

Fold along this line. ▲

After cutting this order form out of the planner along the vertical dotted line, fold it in half along the horizontal line. Please be sure to either complete the payment information on the order form or enclose a check. Then tape the envelope closed along the three open edges. DO NOT SEND CASH.

Use clear tape on all three open sides to seal completely.

Cut along dotted line. ▶

Fête Nationale (Qué.)

FRIDAY 24

*The discovery of a
new dish does more
for the happiness of
mankind than the
discovery of a new star.*
–Anthelme Brillat-Savarin,
French writer (1755–1826)

When the dew is
on the grass, rain will
never come to pass.

SATURDAY 25

In general, harvest
garlic when one-third
to one-half of the
leaves begin to yellow.

SUNDAY 26

REMINDERS

June–July

27 MONDAY

June Holiday (N.L.)
Having more than
120 days of fog per
year, on average,
the Atlantic's
Grand Banks, near
Newfoundland,
is the foggiest place
on Earth.

28 TUESDAY

NEW MOON

29 WEDNESDAY

Don't cross the stream
to find water.
–Swedish proverb

30 THURSDAY

*The glowworms,
numerous, clear,
and bright,
Illumed the dewy
hill last night.*
–attributed to Dr. Erasmus
Darwin, English physician
(1731–1802)

Canada Day
FRIDAY 1

Tides in the Bay of Fundy, between New Brunswick and Nova Scotia, can reach 53 feet—the highest in the world.

SATURDAY 2

The term "garden" stems from the Old English word *"geard,"* which means "enclosure" or "fence."

SUNDAY 3

A friend to everyone is a friend to nobody.

REMINDERS

Complement this planner with daily weather and Almanac wit and wisdom at Almanac.com.

July

**JULY 13:
FULL BUCK MOON**

GOALS AND DREAMS:

_____
_____
_____
_____
_____
_____
_____
_____
_____
_____
_____
_____
_____

*I know who I was
when I got up this
morning, but I think
I must have been
changed several
times since then.*
–Alice in *Alice's
Adventures in
Wonderland,* by
Lewis Carroll, English
writer (1832–98)

SUNDAY	MONDAY	TUESDAY
3	4 *Independence Day*	5
10	11	12
17	18	19
24 / 31	25	26

TUNE IN TO YOUR SENSES.

WEDNESDAY	THURSDAY	FRIDAY	SATURDAY
		1 *Canada Day*	2
6	7	8	9
13	14	15	16
20	21	22	23 *National Day of the Cowboy*
27	28	29 *First of Muharram begins at sundown*	30

JULY

For more holidays and Moon phases, see the weekly pages that follow.

July

4 MONDAY

Independence Day

On July 2, 1776, the Second Continental Congress formally declared independence from Great Britain, but it took 2 days to prepare the official document.

5 TUESDAY

Heat wave? Spicy food induces sweating, which can help you to feel cooler.

6 WEDNESDAY

FIRST QUARTER

7 THURSDAY

Nothing is so firmly believed as what is least known.

–Michel de Montaigne, French essayist (1533–92)

Beginning on this day in 1950, York, Nebraska, received 13.15 inches of rain in 24 hours.

FRIDAY 8

Nunavut Day (Canada)

Baffin Island, the largest in Canada, is in Nunavut, the country's largest territory.

SATURDAY 9

Stop thinking of sweet foods as rewards. Instead, treat yourself to a hot bath, funny movie, long walk, or something else that makes you feel good.

SUNDAY 10

REMINDERS

July

11 MONDAY

Orangemen's Day, observed (N.L.)

If I had to choose just one plant for the whole herb garden, I should be content with basil.
–Elizabeth David, English food writer (1913–92)

12 TUESDAY

The 250,000 or so sweat glands in a person's feet can produce ½ pint of sweat per day.

13 WEDNESDAY

FULL BUCK MOON

14 THURSDAY

To go fishing is the chance to wash one's soul with pure air.
–Herbert Clark Hoover, 31st U.S. president (1874–1964)

Peanuts are legumes,
not nuts. They
are related to lentils
and beans.

FRIDAY 15

*In the end, it's not
the years in your life
that count. It's the
life in your years.*
–Unknown

SATURDAY 16

Meerkats sleep in
piles, keeping the
alphas (the dominant
pair) in the middle,
away from danger.

SUNDAY 17

REMINDERS

July

18 MONDAY

People who keep journals have life twice.
–Jessamyn West,
American writer (1902–84)

19 TUESDAY

It is lucky to have a
left-handed pitcher on
your baseball team.

20 WEDNESDAY

LAST QUARTER

21 THURSDAY

To remove aphids
feeding on collard
leaves, knock them
off with a strong
spray of water.

Jupiter completes one rotation in just under 10 hours, making it the fastest-spinning planet in our solar system.

FRIDAY 22

National Day of the Cowboy

When a cow tries to scratch her ear, It means a shower is very near.

SATURDAY 23

Pioneer Day (Utah)

In order to live off of a garden, you practically have to live in it.
–"Kin" Hubbard, American humorist (1868–1930)

SUNDAY 24

REMINDERS

July

25 MONDAY

The faster a cricket chirps, the warmer the temperature.

26 TUESDAY

On this day in 1775, Benjamin Franklin became the first U.S. postmaster general.

27 WEDNESDAY

Though honey is sweet, do not lick it off a bear.

28 THURSDAY

NEW MOON

**First of Muharram
begins at sundown**

The Moon is moving
about 1.5 inches
farther away from
Earth each year.

FRIDAY 29

The two white
"strings" in an egg
are the chalazae,
which anchor the yolk
(one on each side) to
the shell, protecting
it. Their presence
indicates a fresh egg.

SATURDAY 30

A good lie finds more
believers than a bad truth.

SUNDAY 31

REMINDERS

August

GOALS AND DREAMS:

_____
_____
_____
_____
_____
_____
_____
_____
_____
_____
_____
_____
_____
_____
_____
_____
_____

*Just for today,
I will be happy. . . .
If my mind fills with
clouds, I will chase
them away and fill
it with sunshine.*

–Abigail Van Buren,
American advice
columnist (1918–2013)

SUNDAY	MONDAY	TUESDAY
	1 *Civic Holiday (Canada)*	2
7	8	9
14	15	16
21	22	23
28	29	30

MEDITATE TO REDUCE YOUR STRESS LEVEL AND FOCUS YOUR MIND.

WEDNESDAY	THURSDAY	FRIDAY	SATURDAY
3	4	5	6
10	11	12	13
17	18	19 *National Aviation Day*	20
24	25	26 *Women's Equality Day*	27
31			

For more holidays and Moon phases, see the weekly pages that follow.

August

1 MONDAY

**Colorado Day
Civic Holiday (Canada)**

The state tree of Colorado is the Colorado blue spruce *(Picea pungens),* which botanist Charles C. Parry discovered on Pikes Peak in 1862.

2 TUESDAY

To make scaling fish easier, first rub vinegar onto the scales and let sit for about 5 minutes.

3 WEDNESDAY

You grow up the day you have your first real laugh—at yourself.
–Ethel Barrymore, American actress (1879–1959)

4 THURSDAY

A fallen pinecone left outside on the porch will open in good weather and close in bad.

FRIDAY 5

FIRST QUARTER

SATURDAY 6

Dragonflies can
fly at speeds up to
35 miles per hour.

SUNDAY 7

In ancient
Greek, "iris" means
"rainbow."

REMINDERS

August

8 MONDAY

If one is lucky, a solitary fantasy can totally transform one million realities.

–Maya Angelou, American poet (1928–2014)

9 TUESDAY

Strawberries are not berries, but avocados and bananas are.

10 WEDNESDAY

If your left hand itches, You will get riches.

11 THURSDAY

FULL STURGEON MOON

*It is characteristic
of wisdom not to do
desperate things.*
–Henry David Thoreau,
American writer (1817–62)

FRIDAY 12

Using salt to clean
cast iron pans will
help to remove
stubborn residue and
soak up oils that might
go rancid without
breaking down the
seasoned layer as
soap would do.

SATURDAY 13

*Nothing dries sooner
than a tear.*
–Cicero, Roman
statesman (106–43 B.C.)

SUNDAY 14

AUGUST

REMINDERS

_____

_____

_____

_____

_____

Complement this planner with daily weather and Almanac wit and wisdom at Almanac.com.

August

15 MONDAY

Discovery Day (Y.T.)

To easily peel ginger, use a spoon.

16 TUESDAY

Bennington Battle Day (Vt.)

Keep children, pets, and livestock away from buttercups. Exposure to crushed blossoms can cause skin blisters; ingestion of the plant can result in more serious symptoms.

17 WEDNESDAY

There are three main types of galaxies: spiral, irregular, and elliptical.

18 THURSDAY

The most effective way to do it is to do it.
–Amelia Earhart, American aviatrix (1897–1937)

LAST QUARTER

National Aviation Day

A hard-boiled
egg will spin faster
than a raw one.

AUGUST

Rainbow at noon,
More rain soon.

REMINDERS

22 MONDAY

A house without books is like a room without windows.
–Horace Mann, American educator (1796–1859)

23 TUESDAY

Compost should be watered during dry periods so that it can remain active.

24 WEDNESDAY

You see much more of your children once they leave home.
–Lucille Ball, American comedienne (1911–89)

25 THURSDAY

The horn of a rhinoceros is made mainly of keratin, the same protein found in hair.

Women's Equality Day

FRIDAY **26**

*Make the most of
yourself by fanning the
tiny inner sparks of
possibility into flames
of achievement.*

–Golda Meir, Israeli
politician (1898–1978)

SATURDAY **27**

NEW MOON

SUNDAY **28**

A dream of hurrying
often foretells a change in
the weather.

REMINDERS

29 MONDAY

I'm living so far beyond my income that we may almost be said to be living apart.
–Hector Hugh Munro (aka "Saki"), Scottish writer (1870–1916)

30 TUESDAY

Giraffes sleep for no longer than 5 minutes at a time and for as little as 4 hours in an entire day.

31 WEDNESDAY

Patience is a bitter plant, but it has sweet fruit.
–German proverb

1 THURSDAY

The 2023 Old Farmer's Almanac is available now

Sloths may take
up to 30 days
to digest a meal.

FRIDAY 2

SATURDAY 3

FIRST QUARTER

A Linde star is a
synthetic star sapphire
first made in 1947 by
the Linde Air Products
Company (later a
division of Union
Carbide Corporation).
To check authenticity,
look for an "L"
stamped on the back.

SUNDAY 4

AUGUST

REMINDERS

September

**SEPTEMBER 10:
FULL HARVEST MOON**

GOALS AND DREAMS:

_Go forth under
the open sky, and list
To Nature's
teachings._
–William Cullen Bryant,
American poet
(1794–1878)

SUNDAY	MONDAY	TUESDAY
4	5 _Labor Day_	6
11 _Patriot Day_ _Grandparents Day_	12	13
18	19	20
25 _Rosh Hashanah begins_ _at sundown_	26	27

TAKE A CLASS TO LEARN A NEW LANGUAGE OR SKILL.

WEDNESDAY	THURSDAY	FRIDAY	SATURDAY
	1	2	3
7	8	9	10
14	15	16	17 *Constitution Day*
21 *International Day of Peace*	22 *Autumnal Equinox*	23	24
28	29	30	

For more holidays and Moon phases, see the weekly pages that follow.

September

5 MONDAY

Books can not be killed by fire.
–Franklin D. Roosevelt, 32nd U.S. president (1882–1945)

6 TUESDAY

For healthy skin, eat a handful of almonds every day.

7 WEDNESDAY

I have not failed. I've just found 10,000 ways that won't work.
–Thomas Edison, American inventor (1847–1931)

8 THURSDAY

A lower price for a certain brand does not always mean a greater bargain. Compare the price per ounce among grocery items: Look for the most product for the least expense.

Admission Day (Calif.)

FRIDAY 9

Hulda Crooks
climbed California's
Mt. Whitney 23 times
between the ages of
66 and 91 (in 1962–87),
earning the nickname
"Grandma Whitney."

SATURDAY 10

FULL HARVEST MOON

Patriot Day
Grandparents Day

SUNDAY 11

Send flowers such
as forget-me-nots
(the official flower of
Grandparents Day)
to Grandma and
Grandpa today.

REMINDERS

Complement this planner with daily weather and Almanac wit and wisdom at Almanac.com.

September

12 MONDAY

To check whether a pineapple is ripe, look for a mostly yellow (not green or orange) exterior; a slightly squeezable texture; and a sweet, fruity (not fermented) aroma.

13 TUESDAY

The first face to appear on the U.S. one-dollar bill (issued in 1862) was that of Salmon P. Chase, U.S. secretary of the treasury.

14 WEDNESDAY

During its lifetime, a cow will produce enough milk to fill nearly 200,000 glasses.

15 THURSDAY

If you watch a game, it's fun. If you play it, it's recreation. If you work at it, it's golf.
–Bob Hope, American comedian (1903–2003)

The U.S. Constitution
was drafted in
fewer than
100 working days.

FRIDAY 16

LAST QUARTER

Constitution Day

SATURDAY 17

Plant new perennials
a month before
the first hard frost
is expected.

SUNDAY 18

SEPTEMBER

REMINDERS

September

19 MONDAY

Every human has a unique tongue print as well as distinguishing fingerprints.

20 TUESDAY

When the finch chirps, rain follows.

21 WEDNESDAY

International Day of Peace

Prayers, peace walks, and acts of kindness are some of the many ways to celebrate peace on this day.

22 THURSDAY

Autumnal Equinox

Now Autumn's fire burns slowly along the woods.
–William Allingham, Irish poet (1824–89)

Walruses can
sleep both on land
and at sea.

FRIDAY 23

Keep centerpieces
low so that guests
can see each other
across the table.

SATURDAY 24

SUNDAY 25

NEW MOON

**Rosh Hashanah
begins at sundown**

REMINDERS

26 MONDAY

Rosh Hashanah,
the Jewish New Year,
begins 10 days of
reflection and prayer.

27 TUESDAY

The morning is wiser
than the evening.
–Russian proverb

28 WEDNESDAY

*He was a bold
man who first
swallowed an oyster.*
–James I, British monarch
(1566–1625)

29 THURSDAY

A little nonsense
now and then
Is relished by the
wisest men.

On Saturn, winds
blow at up to 1,100
miles per hour.

FRIDAY 30

He who holds the ladder
is as bad as the thief.

SATURDAY 1

SUNDAY 2

FIRST QUARTER

REMINDERS

Complement this planner with daily weather and Almanac wit and wisdom at Almanac.com.

October

GOALS AND DREAMS:

_____
_____
_____
_____
_____
_____
_____
_____
_____
_____
_____
_____
_____
_____
_____
_____
_____
_____

*Honesty is the
first chapter in the
book of wisdom.*

–Thomas Jefferson,
3rd U.S. president
(1743–1826)

SUNDAY	MONDAY	TUESDAY
2	3 *Child Health Day*	4 *Yom Kippur begins at sundown*
9 *Leif Eriksson Day*	10 *Columbus Day, observed* *Indigenous Peoples' Day* *Thanksgiving Day (Canada)*	11
16	17	18
23	24 *United Nations Day*	25
30	31 *Halloween*	

BE HONEST WITH YOURSELF: CONNECT TO YOUR CORE TRUTH AND VALUES.

WEDNESDAY	THURSDAY	FRIDAY	SATURDAY
			1
5	6	7	8
12 *National Farmer's Day*	13	14	15
19	20	21	22
26	27	28	29

For more holidays and Moon phases, see the weekly pages that follow.

October

3 MONDAY

Child Health Day

Make healthy snacks
more appealing
to kids by presenting
them in fun shapes.

4 TUESDAY

**Yom Kippur begins
at sundown**

*Where there is
great love, there are
always miracles.*

–Willa Cather, American
writer (1873–1947)

5 WEDNESDAY

The Asian tiger snake
is the only serpent
in the world that is
both venomous (toxins
delivered by injection)
and poisonous
(toxins delivered via
touch, inhalation,
or ingestion).

6 THURSDAY

A tree is known
by its fruit,
not by its leaves.

The truth is always exciting. Speak it, then. Life is dull without it.
–Pearl S. Buck, American writer (1892–1973)

FRIDAY 7

On this day in 1901, the city of Galveston, Texas, received 12 inches of rain in just 6 hours.

SATURDAY 8

FULL HUNTER'S MOON

Leif Eriksson Day

SUNDAY 9

REMINDERS

October

10 MONDAY

Columbus Day, observed
Indigenous Peoples' Day
Thanksgiving Day
(Canada)

South Dakota was
the first U.S. state
to celebrate Native
Americans' Day as an
official state holiday.

11 TUESDAY

More than
129 million different
book titles have
been published.

12 WEDNESDAY

National Farmer's Day

A worker honeybee
will produce only 1/12
teaspoon of honey
during its lifetime.

13 THURSDAY

According to some
experts, the shortest
complete sentence
in the English
language is "I am."

When your work speaks for itself, don't interrupt.
–Henry J. Kaiser, American industrialist (1882–1967)

FRIDAY 14

A sunshiny shower
Won't last half an hour.

SATURDAY 15

The average meteoroid is smaller than an apple seed.

SUNDAY 16

REMINDERS

October

17 MONDAY

LAST QUARTER

18 TUESDAY

Alaska Day

In 1996, a 459-pound
Pacific halibut was
caught in Unalaska
Bay, Alaska, setting
a world record.

19 WEDNESDAY

*Education is not the
filling of a pail, but the
lighting of a fire.*
–attributed to William
Butler Yeats, Irish poet
(1865–1939)

20 THURSDAY

When roasting
vegetables, putting
too many in the pan
can cause them to
steam instead of
roast, creating mushy,
flavorless results.
Keep to a single layer,
with about ¼ inch
between vegetables.

The more black (and less brown) on the banded woolly bear caterpillar, the more severe the coming winter will be.

FRIDAY 21

No book is of much importance; the vital thing is, What do you yourself think?
–Elbert Hubbard, American writer (1856–1915)

SATURDAY 22

Potatoes were first cultivated about 8,000 years ago, in Peru.

SUNDAY 23

REMINDERS

Complement this planner with daily weather and Almanac wit and wisdom at Almanac.com.

October

24 MONDAY

United Nations Day

*Look up, and not down;
look forward, and
not back; look out, and
not in; and lend a hand.*

–Edward Everett Hale,
American clergyman
(1822–1909)

25 TUESDAY

NEW MOON

**Partial Solar Eclipse
(not visible in N.Am.)**

26 WEDNESDAY

*The road to ruin
is always kept in
good repair.*

–Josh Billings, American
humorist (1818–85)

27 THURSDAY

In some cultures, a
child's newly shed
"baby" tooth is tossed
up toward the Sun
in celebration.

Nevada Day

Nevada is the leading
gold producer in
the United States
and one of the largest
sources of the
element in the world.

FRIDAY 28

If crows fly low,
winds going to blow;
If crows fly high,
winds going to die.

SATURDAY 29

The small inner
pocket on jeans was
originally meant for
pocket watches.

SUNDAY 30

REMINDERS

OCTOBER

Complement this planner with daily weather and Almanac wit and wisdom at Almanac.com.

November

NOVEMBER 8:
FULL BEAVER MOON

GOALS AND DREAMS:

_____
_____
_____
_____
_____
_____
_____
_____
_____
_____
_____
_____
_____
_____
_____
_____
_____
_____
_____
_____

Gratitude is the
memory of the heart.
–Jean Massieu, French
educator (1772–1846)

SUNDAY	MONDAY	TUESDAY
		1
6 *Daylight Saving Time ends at 2:00 A.M.*	7	8 *Election Day*
13	14	15
20 *National Child Day (Canada)*	21	22
27	28	29

SET ASIDE SOME TIME TO THINK ABOUT THINGS FOR WHICH YOU ARE GRATEFUL.

WEDNESDAY	THURSDAY	FRIDAY	SATURDAY
2	3	4	5
9	10 *U.S. Marine Corps Birthday*	11 *Veterans Day Remembrance Day (Canada)*	12
16	17	18	19 *Discovery of Puerto Rico Day*
23	24 *Thanksgiving Day*	25	26
30			

For more holidays and Moon phases, see the weekly pages that follow.

NOVEMBER

October–November

31 MONDAY

Halloween
Goblins beware . . .
of traffic! Wear
reflector tape and
carry a flashlight.

1 TUESDAY

FIRST QUARTER

2 WEDNESDAY

If you want to dream
of your intended,
put thyme in one shoe and
rosemary in the other.

3 THURSDAY

Before frying, sprinkle
salt or flour in the
skillet to prevent hot
oil from splattering.

Will Rogers Day (Okla.)

FRIDAY 4

We can't all be heroes, because somebody has to sit on the curb and applaud when they go by.

–Will Rogers, American actor (1879–1935)

SATURDAY 5

When making a layer cake, cool the cake layers upside down to flatten the tops.

Daylight Saving Time ends at 2:00 A.M.

SUNDAY 6

Time is the wisest counselor.

–Pericles, Greek statesman (c. 495–429 B.C.)

REMINDERS

November

7 MONDAY

On this day in 1951, people in parts of Kansas, Oklahoma, and Texas saw a flash and ball of fire as a meteor disintegrated in the atmosphere.

8 TUESDAY

FULL BEAVER MOON

Election Day
Total Lunar Eclipse (visible in parts of N.Am.)

9 WEDNESDAY

When I was born, I was so surprised I didn't talk for a year and a half.
–Gracie Allen, American comedienne (c. 1895–1964)

10 THURSDAY

U.S. Marine Corps Birthday
Since 1957, several English bulldogs named Chesty (after Lt. Gen. Lewis B. "Chesty" Puller) have served as the mascot of the U.S. Marine Corps.

Veterans Day

Remembrance Day (Canada)

FRIDAY 11

It always seems quite fitting that this day comes deep in autumn when . . . the days seem to invite contemplation.
–Ronald Reagan, 40th U.S. president (1911–2004)

To remove musty smells in the freezer, add a clean sock filled with dry coffee grounds.

SATURDAY 12

If a bird leaves droppings on your left shoulder, you will have good fortune.

SUNDAY 13

REMINDERS

NOVEMBER

November

14 MONDAY

It is better to deserve without receiving than to receive without deserving.
–Robert Green Ingersoll, American lawyer (1833–99)

15 TUESDAY

To shorten cooking time, first soak brown rice overnight.

16 WEDNESDAY

LAST QUARTER

17 THURSDAY

Luck is like having a rice dumpling fly into your mouth.
–Japanese proverb

Be careful: If you are
epileptic or pregnant,
do not consume
large quantities of
sage. Some types
contain thujone,
which in high doses
may cause seizures
or miscarriage.

FRIDAY 18

Discovery of Puerto Rico Day

Q: My inside can
be up to 20 degrees
Fahrenheit cooler
than my outside.
I am 95 percent water.
What am I?

A: Cucumber

SATURDAY 19

National Child Day (Canada)

A small body may
harbor a great soul.

SUNDAY 20

REMINDERS

NOVEMBER

Complement this planner with daily weather and Almanac wit and wisdom at Almanac.com.

November

21 MONDAY

There are over
800 species
of hermit crabs.

22 TUESDAY

Cranberries have
small bubbles of air
inside that allow them
to float in water.

23 WEDNESDAY

NEW MOON

24 THURSDAY

Thanksgiving Day

If you feed a stranger
on Thanksgiving Day,
it will bring good luck.

Acadian Day (La.)

From our viewpoint,
as Earth rotates,
Polaris—aka the
North Star—remains
in place while the
other stars circle
around it.

FRIDAY 25

*Truth is immortal;
error is mortal.*

–Mary Baker Eddy,
American religious leader
(1821–1910)

SATURDAY 26

No weather is ill,
If the wind is still.

SUNDAY 27

REMINDERS

Complement this planner with daily weather and Almanac wit and wisdom at Almanac.com.

28 MONDAY

The arctic tern has the longest migration of any animal, traveling from the Arctic Circle to the Antarctic Circle and back every year.

29 TUESDAY

When baking bread, place a small bowl of water in the oven. The steam helps the dough to rise higher and the crust to be crispy, thin, and slightly glazed.

30 WEDNESDAY

FIRST QUARTER

1 THURSDAY

The eye is the pearl of the face.

The roots of a fig tree
were found in a
cave in South Africa
at a depth of
400 feet—setting a
world record for the
deepest tree roots.

Never put your hand
out farther than you can
draw it back again.
–Irish proverb

Small, unbranched
crystals of ice called
"diamond dust" form
in stable air at bitterly
cold temperatures.
Falling so slowly
that they seem to be
floating in air, they
sparkle when hit by
sunlight or moonlight.

REMINDERS

NOVEMBER

Complement this planner with daily weather and Almanac wit and wisdom at Almanac.com.

December

**DECEMBER 7:
FULL COLD MOON**

GOALS AND DREAMS:

_____
_____
_____
_____
_____
_____
_____
_____
_____
_____
_____
_____
_____
_____
_____
_____

*Have you had a
kindness shown?
Pass it on.
'Twas not given for
thee alone,
Pass it on.*
–Henry Burton, English
clergyman (1840–1930)

SUNDAY	MONDAY	TUESDAY
4	5	6
11	12	13
18	19 *Chanukah begins at sundown*	20
25 *Christmas Day*	26 *Boxing Day (Canada) First day of Kwanzaa*	27

PAY IT FORWARD: CONSIDER WHAT FAVORS YOU MIGHT DO FOR OTHERS TODAY.

WEDNESDAY	THURSDAY	FRIDAY	SATURDAY
	1	2	3
7 *National Pearl Harbor Remembrance Day*	8	9	10
14	15 *Bill of Rights Day*	16	17 *Wright Brothers Day*
21 *Winter Solstice*	22	23	24
28	29	30	31 *New Year's Eve*

For more holidays and Moon phases, see the weekly pages that follow.

December

5 MONDAY

The Roman text *The Ten Books on Architecture (De architectura libri decem)*, written in 27 B.C., is the oldest western manual still intact that addresses garden design.

6 TUESDAY

The Night walked down the sky With the Moon in her hand.
–Frederick Lawrence Knowles, American poet (1869–1905)

7 WEDNESDAY

FULL COLD MOON

National Pearl Harbor Remembrance Day

8 THURSDAY

In trying times, don't quit trying.

I will not follow where the path may lead, but I will go where there is no path, and I will leave a trail.

–Muriel Strode, American poet (1875–1964)

FRIDAY 9

As a general rule, the distance from your elbow to your wrist equals the length of your foot.

SATURDAY 10

Methuselah, a 4,853-year-old Great Basin bristlecone pine, is the oldest living non-clonal organism on Earth that has a confirmed age.

SUNDAY 11

REMINDERS

Complement this planner with daily weather and Almanac wit and wisdom at Almanac.com.

December

12 MONDAY

Beware of a door that has too many keys.

13 TUESDAY

In any culture, approximately 1 person in 10 is left-handed.

14 WEDNESDAY

A dream of a coconut may signify that you'll soon receive an unexpected gift.

15 THURSDAY

Bill of Rights Day

Today, we stand on the shoulders of those who dedicated their lives to upholding the meaning of our founding documents throughout changing times.

–Barack Obama, 44th U.S. president (b. 1961)

LAST QUARTER

FRIDAY 16

Wright Brothers Day

There is no flying
without wings.
–French proverb

SATURDAY 17

**Chanukah begins
at sundown**

*Eight lights we burn
before the shrine,
To celebrate this
feast divine.*
–"The Hanukkah
Lights," 1913

SUNDAY 18

REMINDERS

December

19 MONDAY

There can be more than 12,000 working parts in a piano.

20 TUESDAY

The sun, the open air, silence, and art are great physicians.
–Santiago Ramón y Cajal, Spanish neuroscientist (1852–1934)

21 WEDNESDAY

Winter Solstice

In the Northern Hemisphere, this is the first day of winter and the shortest day of the year. Need warmth? Visit the Southern Hemisphere, where summer is just starting.

22 THURSDAY

A snowflake that falls at a rate of 2 to 4 miles per hour will take around 1 hour to reach the ground.

NEW MOON

FRIDAY 23

On Christmas Eve in Brazil, where it is summer, families often eat dinner late in the evening and exchange gifts. At midnight, many attend mass and enjoy fireworks.

SATURDAY 24

Christmas Day

Do what you can to show you care about other people and you will make our world a better place.

–Rosalynn Carter, U.S. First Lady (b. 1927)

SUNDAY 25

REMINDERS

26 MONDAY

Boxing Day (Canada)
First day of Kwanzaa
The first day of
the 7-day Kwanzaa
celebration embraces
the principle
of *Umoja,* or unity.

27 TUESDAY

*Of course we
weren't lost. We were
merely where we
shouldn't have been
without knowing
where that was.*
–T. Morris Longstreth,
American writer
(1886–1975)

28 WEDNESDAY

'Tis not the matter
but the mind.

29 THURSDAY

FIRST QUARTER

In 2007, New York's *Serendipity 3* restaurant unveiled the Frrrozen Haute Chocolate. At $25,000 per serving, it set a record as the world's most expensive dessert. (All profits went to charities.)

FRIDAY 30

I never think of the future. It comes soon enough.
–Albert Einstein, American physicist (1879–1955)

SATURDAY 31

New Year's Day

This is the beginning of anything you want to do or be.

SUNDAY 1

REMINDERS

Complement this planner with daily weather and Almanac wit and wisdom at Almanac.com.

2023 Advance Planner

bold = *U.S. and/or Canadian national holidays*

JANUARY

S	M	T	W	T	F	S
1	2	3	4	5	6	7
8	9	10	11	12	13	14
15	16	17	18	19	20	21
22	23	24	25	26	27	28
29	30	31				

FEBRUARY

S	M	T	W	T	F	S
			1	2	3	4
5	6	7	8	9	10	11
12	13	14	15	16	17	18
19	20	21	22	23	24	25
26	27	28				

MARCH

S	M	T	W	T	F	S
			1	2	3	4
5	6	7	8	9	10	11
12	13	14	15	16	17	18
19	20	21	22	23	24	25
26	27	28	29	30	31	

APRIL

S	M	T	W	T	F	S
						1
2	3	4	5	6	7	8
9	10	11	12	13	14	15
16	17	18	19	20	21	22
23	24	25	26	27	28	29
30						

MAY

S	M	T	W	T	F	S
	1	2	3	4	5	6
7	8	9	10	11	12	13
14	15	16	17	18	19	20
21	22	23	24	25	26	27
28	29	30	31			

JUNE

S	M	T	W	T	F	S
				1	2	3
4	5	6	7	8	9	10
11	12	13	14	15	16	17
18	19	20	21	22	23	24
25	26	27	28	29	30	

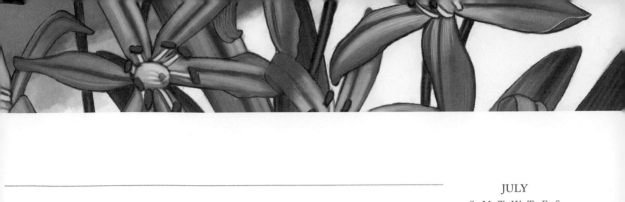

_____
_____
_____
_____
_____
_____
_____
_____
_____
_____
_____
_____
_____
_____
_____
_____
_____
_____
_____
_____
_____
_____
_____
_____
_____
_____
_____
_____
_____
_____
_____
_____
_____

JULY

S	M	T	W	T	F	S
						1
2	3	4	5	6	7	8
9	10	11	12	13	14	15
16	17	18	19	20	21	22
23	24	25	26	27	28	29
30	31					

AUGUST

S	M	T	W	T	F	S
		1	2	3	4	5
6	7	8	9	10	11	12
13	14	15	16	17	18	19
20	21	22	23	24	25	26
27	28	29	30	31		

SEPTEMBER

S	M	T	W	T	F	S
					1	2
3	4	5	6	7	8	9
10	11	12	13	14	15	16
17	18	19	20	21	22	23
24	25	26	27	28	29	30

OCTOBER

S	M	T	W	T	F	S
1	2	3	4	5	6	7
8	9	10	11	12	13	14
15	16	17	18	19	20	21
22	23	24	25	26	27	28
29	30	31				

NOVEMBER

S	M	T	W	T	F	S
			1	2	3	4
5	6	7	8	9	10	11
12	13	14	15	16	17	18
19	20	21	22	23	24	25
26	27	28	29	30		

DECEMBER

S	M	T	W	T	F	S
					1	2
3	4	5	6	7	8	9
10	11	12	13	14	15	16
17	18	19	20	21	22	23
24	25	26	27	28	29	30
31						

Planning a trip? See the Long-Range Weather Forecast at Almanac.com/Weather.

Passwords

WEB SITE	USER NAME	PASSWORD

Contacts

Name _____ Home _____
Address _____ Work _____
_____ Cell _____
Email _____ Fax _____

Name _____ Home _____
Address _____ Work _____
_____ Cell _____
Email _____ Fax _____

Name _____ Home _____
Address _____ Work _____
_____ Cell _____
Email _____ Fax _____

Name _____ Home _____
Address _____ Work _____
_____ Cell _____
Email _____ Fax _____

Name _____ Home _____
Address _____ Work _____
_____ Cell _____
Email _____ Fax _____

Name _____ Home _____
Address _____ Work _____
_____ Cell _____
Email _____ Fax _____

Name _____ Home _____
Address _____ Work _____
_____ Cell _____
Email _____ Fax _____

Emergency Contacts

In case of emergency, notify:

Name:	Home:
Address:	Work:
	Cell:
Relationship:	Email:
Police department:	Gas company:
Fire department:	Electric company:
Ambulance:	Electrician:
Hospital:	Plumber:
Physician:	School(s):
Dentist:	Day care:
Pharmacy:	Baby-sitter:
Poison control:	Veterinarian:
Clergy:	Insurance, auto:
City/town office:	Homeowner's:
Carpenter:	Health:
Auto mechanic:	Dental:
Phone company:	Credit card(s):
Cell provider:	
Internet provider:	Bank:
Cable/satellite company:	
Other:	

THE OLD FARMER'S ALMANAC

For gardening advice, weather forecasts, and more, visit **Almanac.com.**

Thank you for choosing this planner. We hope that you enjoy it!